Dedication

To all those who ever struggled with learning a foreign language and to Wolfgang Karfunkel

Also by Yatir Nitzany

Conversational Spanish Quick and Easy

Conversational French Quick and Easy

Conversational Italian Quick and Easy

Conversational Portuguese Quick and Easy

Conversational German Quick and Easy

Conversational Dutch Quick and Easy

Conversational Norwegian Quick and Easy

Conversational Danish Quick and Easy

Conversational Russian Quick and Easy

Conversational Ukrainian Quick and Easy

Conversational Bulgarian Quick and Easy

Conversational Polish Quick and Easy

Conversational Hebrew Quick and Easy

Conversational Yiddish Quick and Easy

Conversational Armenian Quick and Easy

Conversational Arabic Quick and Easy

Conversational Hebrew Quick and Easy
The Most Innovative Technique to Learn the Hebrew Language

Part III

YATIR NITZANY

Translated by:
Semadar Mercedes Friedman

Interior Design:
Menachem Otto

Copyright © 2019
Yatir Nitzany
All rights reserved.
ISBN 13: 978-1951244507
Printed in the United States of America

Foreword

About Myself

For many years I struggled to learn Spanish, and I still knew no more than about twenty words. Consequently, I was extremely frustrated. One day I stumbled upon this method as I was playing around with word combinations. Suddenly, I came to the realization that every language has a certain core group of words that are most commonly used and, simply by learning them, one could gain the ability to engage in quick and easy conversational Spanish.

I discovered which words those were, and I narrowed them down to three hundred and fifty that, once memorized, one could connect and create one's own sentences. The variations were and are *infinite*! By using this incredibly simple technique, I could converse at a proficient level and speak Spanish. Within a week, I astonished my Spanish-speaking friends with my newfound ability. The next semester I registered at my university for a Spanish language course, and I applied the same principles I had learned in that class (grammar, additional vocabulary, future and past tense, etc.) to those three hundred and fifty words I already had memorized, and immediately I felt as if I had grown wings and learned how to fly.

At the end of the semester, we took a class trip to San José, Costa Rica. I was like a fish in water, while the rest of my classmates were floundering and still struggling to converse. Throughout the following months, I again applied the same principle to other languages—French, Portuguese, Italian, and Arabic, all of which I now speak proficiently, thanks to this very simple technique.

This method is by far the fastest way to master quick and easy conversational language skills. There is no other technique that compares to my concept. It is effective, it worked for me, and it will work for you. Be consistent with my program, and you too will succeed the way I and many, many others have.

Table of Contents

Introduction to the Program 9

Introduction to the Hebrew Language 11

Memorization Made Easy...12

Hebrew Pronunciation 13

The Program

- Office... 15
- School.. 19
- Profession 21
- Business 25
- Sports 29
- Outdoor Activities 33
- Electric... 35
- Tools 37
- Auto 41
- Nature 43
- Animals 45
- Religion 49
- Wedding and Relationship 53
- Politics 49
- Military 53

Basic Grammatical Requirements of the Hebrew Language...................57

Conclusion...63

Note from the Author 64

Introduction to the Program

You have now reached Part 3 of Conversational Hebrew Quick and Easy. In Part 1 you learned the 350 words that could be used in an infinite number of combinations. In Part 2 you moved on to putting these words into sentences. You learned how to ask for help when your house was hit by a hurricane and how to find the emergency services. For example, if you need to go to a hospital, you have now been provided with sentences and the vocabulary for talking to doctors and nurses and dealing with surgery and health issues. When you get to the hospital, you can tell the health services, "The hurricane caused a lot of destruction and damage in its path," and "We used the hurricane shelter for refuge."

In this third book in the series, you will find the culmination of this foreign language course that is based on a system using key phrases used in day-to-day life. You can now move on to further topics such as things you would say in an office. This theme is ideal if you've just moved to Hebrew for a new job. You may be about to sit at your desk to do an important task assigned to you by your boss but you have forgotten the details you were given. Turn to your colleagues and say, "I have to write an important email but I forgot my password." Then, if the reply is "Our secretary isn't here today. Only the receptionist is here but she is in the bathroom," you'll know what is being said and you can wait for help. By the end of the first few weeks, you'll have at your disposal terminology that can help reflect your experiences. "I want to retire already," you may find yourself saying at coffee break on a Monday morning after having had to go to your bank manager and say, "I need a small loan in order to pay my mortgage this month."

I came up with the idea of this unique system of learning foreign languages as I was struggling with my own attempt to learn Hebrew. When playing around with word combinations I discovered 350 words that when used together could make up an infinite number of sentences. From this beginning, I was able to start speaking in a new language. I then practiced and found that I could use the same technique with other languages, such as French, Portuguese, Italian and Arabic. It was a revelation.

This method is by far the easiest and quickest way to master other languages and begin practicing conversational language skills.

The range of topics and the core vocabulary are the main components of this flawless learning method. In Part 3 you have a chance to learn how to relate to people in many more ways. Sports, for example, are very important for keeping healthy and in good spirits. The social component of these types of activities should not be underestimated at all. You will, therefore, have much help when you meet some new people, perhaps in a bar, and want to say to them, "I like to watch basketball games," and "Today are the finals of the Olympic Games. Let's see who wins the World Cup."

For sports, the office, and for school, some parts of conversation are essential. What happens when you need to get to work but don't have any clean clothes to wear because of malfunctions with the machinery. What you need is to be able to pick up the phone and ask a professional or a friend, "My washing machine and dryer are broken so maybe I can wash my laundry at the public laundromat." When you finally head out after work for some drinks and meet a nice new man, you can say, "You can leave me a voicemail or send me a text message."

Hopefully, these examples help show you how reading all three parts of this series in combination will prepare you for all you need in order to boost your conversational learning skills and engage with others in your newly learned language. The first two books have been an important start. This third book adds additional vocabulary and will provide the comprehensive knowledge required.

The Hebrew Language

The two most ancient written cultures in the world (other than Egyptian with its hieroglyphics) are Chinese in the Far East and Hebrew in the Middle East. Abraham, the father of the three monotheistic faiths, was the first person to speak Hebrew, and the book to introduce his story is the Bible. This awesome literary work covers thousands of years of history, and the book is translated into 126 languages. Hebrew further developed from generation to generation, and its vocabulary became more extensive.

For three millenniums, great works of Hebrew scholars were written in Hebrew and translated into many languages; works such as the Mishna, Talmud, Haggadah, and Derash.

Great philosophers, such as Saadia Gaon (around 800 C.E.) and Rabbi Moses Ben Maimon—known as Maimonides—in the twelfth century, also wrote their philosophies in Hebrew and Arabic (the lingua franca of this historical period). Their works were then translated into Latin and many other languages.

In the medieval era, there were well-known scholars, poets, and authors in Spain, such as Yehuda Halevy, Iben Ezra, Iben Gavirol, and a large number of other writers who expressed themselves in Hebrew.

The Torah, known as the Five Books of Moses in the Bible, was translated into a more comprehensive Hebrew with commentaries by Rashi (a famous rabbi). His native language was French.

In the Enlightenment era, since the great Jewish philosopher Moses Mendelssohn, as well the national poet of Israel, Hayim Nechman Bialik, who expressed himself in the most eloquent Hebrew, creating and adopting it into a modern language and creating new words. Ben Yehuda, who wrote the modern Hebrew dictionary, together with hundreds of writers and superb poets, such as Shaul Tchernichovsky, left an exquisite legacy of literary works in Hebrew. Yet for none of them, Hebrew was their mother tongue. At that time, the language was considered a dead language.

In 1969, Shay Agnon was awarded the Nobel Prize in literature. He wrote in Hebrew, and most of his books are translated into many other languages.

In America, from the Pilgrims' times until 1929, no student was accepted into any Ivy League University, such as Harvard or Yale, unless they read and wrote Hebrew. Most Ivy League universities in the US have a Hebrew Department for Biblical history and the literature of Hebrew scripts. Nowadays, even at the Universities of Tokyo in Japan and Seoul in South Korea, there are Hebrew departments where Hebrew is taught.

In Israel, where the Hebrew language is the national language, there is the Academy of the Hebrew Language, which assists new learners of the language anytime.

Memorization Made Easy

There is no doubt the three hundred and fifty words in my program are the required essentials in order to engage in quick and easy basic conversation in any foreign language. However, some people may experience difficulty in the memorization. For this reason, I created Memorization Made Easy. This memorization technique will make this program so simple and fun that it's unbelievable! I have spread the words over the following twenty pages. Each page contains a vocabulary table of ten to fifteen words. Below every vocabulary box, sentences are composed from the words on the page that you have just studied. This aids greatly in memorization. Once you succeed in memorizing the first page, then proceed to the second page. Upon completion of the second page, go back to the first and review. Then proceed to the third page. After memorizing the third, go back to the first and second and repeat. And so on. As you continue, begin to combine words and create your own sentences in your head. Every time you proceed to the following page, you will notice words from the previous pages will be present in those simple sentences as well, because repetition is one of the most crucial aspects in learning any foreign language. Upon completion of your twenty pages, *congratulations,* you have absorbed the required words and gained a basic, quick-and-easy proficiency and you should now be able to create your own sentences and say anything you wish in the Hebrew language. This is a crash course in conversational Hebrew, and it works!

Reading and Pronunciation

*For Middle Eastern languages, including Hebrew, Arabic, Farsi, Pashto, Urdu, Hindi, etc., and also German, to properly pronounce the *kh* or *ch* is essential, for example, *Chanukah* (a Jewish holiday) or *Khaled* (a Muslim name) or *Nacht* ("night" in German). The best way to describe *kh* or *ch* is to say "ka" or "ha" while at the same time putting your tongue at the back of your throat and blowing air. It's pronounced similarly to the sound that you make while clearing your throat of phlegm.

*In Hebrew, the accent *aa'yin* is pronounced as 'aa, and is pronounced deep at the back of your throat, rather similar to the sound one would make when gagging. In the program, the symbol for *ayin* is 'aa or 'oo.

Ha is pronounced as "ha." Pronunciation takes place deep at the back of your throat, and for correct pronunciation one must constrict the back of the throat and exhale air while simultaneously saying "ha." In the program, this strong *h* ("ha") is emphasized whenever *ah, ha, eh, he,* and *oh* is encountered.

OFFICE - MISRAD

Boss - (male/zachar) Ba'al ha esek / **(female/nekeva)** ba'alat ha esek
Employee - Sachiir / **(female)** schiira
Staff - Tzevet
Meeting - Mifgash / pgisha
Conference room - Chadar yeshivot
Secretary - Maskira / **Receptionist -** Pkidat kabala
Schedule - Luach ha zmaniim / maharechet ha zmaniim
Calendar - Luach ha shana
Supplies - Tziyood
Pen - Ett / **Ink -** Di'yo
Pencil - Eeparon / **Eraser -** Mochek
Desk - Machteva / **Cubicle -** Ta
Chair - Kees'ei
Office furniture - Ri'hoot misradee
Business card - Kartiis asakiim
Lunch break - Afsakat tzo'hora'eem
Days off - Yamei choofsha
Briefcase - Yalkoot mismacheem
Bathroom - Sherootim

My boss asked me to hand in the paperwork.
Ha menahel bikesh mimeni lehageesh lo et ha nayeret.
Our secretary isn't here today. The receptionist is here but she is in the bathroom.
Ha mazkira shelano lo kan hayom. Pkidat-ha kabala kan aval hee ba sherootim.
The employee meeting can take place in the conference room.
Pg'ishat ha ovdiim yechola lehitkayem (to take place) ba chadar ha yeshiv'ott.
My business cards are inside my briefcase.
Kartisei ha asakiim sheli hem bae yalkoot ha mismacheem sheli.
The office staff must check their work schedule daily.
Tzevet hamisrad chayav livdok et maharechet ha zmaniim shel ha avoda midei (each) yom.
I am going to buy office furniture.
Ani **(male)**olech/**(female)**olechet liknot ri'hoot misradee.
There isn't any ink in this pen.
Eiin di'yo ba ett hazei.
This pencil is missing an eraser.
La eeparon hazei chaser (missing) mochek.
Our days off are written on the calendar.
Yamei ha choofsha shelanu ktoovim (are written) al luach ha shana.
I need to buy extra office supplies.
Ani **(male)**tzarich/**(female)**tzreicha liknot tziyood misradee nosaf (extra).
I am busy until my lunch break.
Ani asook/asooka aad afsakat ha tzo'hora'iim.

Laptop - Mach'shev nayad
Computer - Mach'shev
Keyboard - Makledet
Mouse - Achbar
Email - Email / doo'el (do'ar electron'ee)
Password - Sisma
Attachment - Kovetz-metzoraf
Printer - Matpeset
Colored printer - Matpeset tziv'oniit
To download - Lehorid
To upload - Le'ha'alot
Internet - Internet
Account - Cheshbon
A copy - Ha'etek / **To copy** - Leha'ateek
Paste - Lehadbeek
Fax - Fax
Scanner - Sorek / **To scan** - Lisrok
Telephone - Teléfon
Charger - Matt'en / **To charge** (a phone) - Lehat'een

I want to write an important email but I forgot my password for my account.
Ani **(m)**rotzei/**(f)**rotza lichtov email chashoov (important) aval shachachtee et ha sisma shel ha cheshbon sheli.
I need to purchase a computer, a keyboard, a printer, and a desk.
Ani tzarich/tzreicha liknot machshev, makledet, matpeset, ve machteva.
Where is the mouse on my laptop?
Eifo ha achbar shel ha machshev ha nayad sheli?
The internet is slow today therefore it's difficult to upload or download.
Ha internet eetii (slow) hayom ve-lachen (and therefore) kashei le'ha'alot hoo lehoreed.
Do you have a colored printer?
Yesh (m)lecha/(f)lach matpeset tziv'oneet?
I needed to fax the contract but instead, I decided to send it as an attachment in the email.
Ani hayiti tzarich/tzreicha lefakses et ha chozei aval bimkom hechlateti lishloach oto ke-kovetz-metzoraf la email.
One day, the fax machine will be completely obsolete.
Yom echad mechonat ha faks teehe'yae pasool (obsolete) lechalooteen (completely).
Where is my phone charger?
Eifo mat'hen ha telefon sheli?
The scanner is broken.
Ha sorek shavoor (broken).
The telephone is behind the chair.
Ha telefon nimtza me'achorei (behind) ha kisei.

Office

Shredder - Magrasa
Copy machine - Mechonat tzi'loom / mechonat ha'atakah
Filing cabinet - A'ron tiyook
Paper - Neyar, **(p)** Neyarot / **Page** - Daaf, **(p)** dappiim
Paperwork - Nayeret
Portfolio - Oogdan
Files - Kvatzim
Document - Mismach
Contract - Chozae
Records - Reshimot
Archives - Archyoon
Deadline - Mo'ed acharon
Binder - Ogdan
Paper clip - Atav nee'yar
Stapler - Mahadek / **Staples** - Mehadkeem
Stamp - Bool
Mail - Do'ar
Letter - Michtav
Envelope - Ma'atafa
Data - Da'ta / maydaa
Analysis - Neetoo'ach
Highlighter - Ett sim'oon / **Marker** - Mesamen / **To highlight** - Lesamen
Ruler - Sarg'el

The supervisor at our company is responsible for data analysis.
Mefakei'ach ha chevra shelanoo achra'ee al neetoo'ach ha maydaa.
The copy machine is next to the telephone.
Mechonat ha tziloom leyad (next to) ha telefon.
I can't find my stapler, paper clips, nor my highlighter in my cubicle.
Ani lo yachol limtzo et ha mehadek, et ha sikot, ve lo et ett ha sim'oon sheli ba ta sheli.
The filing cabinet is full of documents.
A'ron ha tiyook malei-bei (full of) mismachiim.
The garbage can is full.
Paach ha ashpa malei.
Give me the file because today is the deadline.
Ten-lee (give me) et ha teek ki hayom hoo ha mohed ha acharon.
Where do I put the binder?
Eefo laseem et ha oogdan?
The ruler is next to the shredder.
Ha sarg'el nimtza leyad ha magresa.
I need a stamp and an envelope.
Ani tzarich/treicha bool hoo mahatafa.
There is a letter in the mail.
Yesh michtav ba do'ar.

SCHOOL - BEIT SEFER

Student - Talmid **/ (f)** talmida **/ (p)** talmidiim
Teacher - Morei **/ (f)** mora
Substitute teacher - Memalei makom
A class - Shihoor
A classroom - Keeta
Education - Chinooch
Private school - Beit sefer prati
Public school - Beit sefer tziboori
Elementary school - Beit sefer yesodee
Middle school - Chativat beiy'nay'eem
High school - Beit sefer tichon
University - Ooniversita **/ College -** Michlala
Grade (level) **-** Kita **/ Grade** (grade on a test) **-** Tzi'yoon
Pass - Avar **/ Fail -** Nichshal
Absent - Chaser
Present - Nochach

The classroom is empty.
Ha kita reika (empty).
I want to bring my laptop to class.
Ani rotzei lahavi eeti (with me) et machshev ha nayad sheli la kita.
Our math teacher is absent and therefore a substitute teacher replaced him.
Ha morei shelano le matematica lo kan hayom ve lachen mora ha machlifa hechlifa oto.
All the students are present.
Kol ha talmidiim nochaciim.
Make sure to pass your classes because you can't fail this semester.
Tid'ag (make sure) lahavor et kol ha kitoot shelcha mikevan shae ata lo yachol leikashel ba samester hazei.
The education level at a private school is much more intense.
Ramat ha chinooch bae beit sefer prati arbei yoter intensivit.
I went to a public elementary and middle school.
Lamadeti bae beit sefer yesodi tzibori ve bae chativat beiy'nay'eem tzibori.
I have good memories of high school.
Yesh li zichronot (memories) tovot mei beit ha sefer tichon.
My son is 15 years old and he is in the ninth grade.
Ha ben sheli ben-chameshesrei (15 years old) ve hoo bae kita tet (ninth).
You must get good grades on your report card.
Aleicha lekabel tziyoniim toviim ba tehuda shelcha.
College textbooks are expensive.
Sifrei limood ba michlala em yekariim (expensive).
I want to study at an out-of-state university.
Ani rotzei/rotza lilmod bae universita mechootz-la (outside of) medina.

Subject - Nos'ae
Science - Mada / **Chemistry** - Cheem'ee'ya / **Physics** - Physica
Geography - Guio'grafi'ya
History - Histor'ya
Math - Matemática / cheshbon
Addition - Chiboor
Subtraction - Chisoor
Division - Chilook
Multiplication - Kefel
Language - Safa / **English** - Anglit / **Foreign language** - Safa zara
Physical education - Shi'oor eetamloot
Chalk - G'iir / **Board** - Luach
Report card - Tehuda
Alphabet - Alef-bet / **Letters** - Oti'yot / **Words** - Mi'leem
To review - Lachzor al
Dictionary - Milon
Detention - Reetook
The principle - Menahel / **(f)** menahelet

At school, geography is my favorite class, English is easy, math is hard, and history is boring.
Bae beit ha sefer guio'grafi'ya ha shihoor ha hahoov (favorite) alai, anglit kal, matematika kashei, ve historya meshahamem (boring).
After English class, there is physical education.
Achrei shihoor anglit yesh itamloot.
Today's math lesson is on addition and subtraction. Next month it will be division and multiplication.
Shihoor ha matematika hayom mevusas-al (based on) chiboor ve chisoor. Ba chodesh (month) haba (next) chilook ve kifool.
This year for foreign language credits, I want to choose Spanish and French.
Ha shana havoor nekudat-zchoot ba safa zara, ani rotzei lilmod sfaradiit ve tzarfateet.
I want to buy a dictionary, thesaurus, and a journal for school.
Ani rotzei/rotza liknot milon, tzoroos, ve yoman la limoodiim.
The teacher needs to write the homework on the board with chalk.
Ha morei tzarich lichtov et ha shihoorei bait bei giir al ha luach.
Today the students have to review the letters of the alphabet.
Hayom ha talmidiim chayaviim lachzor al otiyoot ha alef bet.
The teacher wants to teach the students roman numerals.
Ha mora rotza leilamed et ha talmidiim ba sfarot romiyot.
If you can't behave well then you must go to the principal's office, and maybe stay after school for detention.
Eem ata lo yachol leihtnaheg yafei az alecha lageshet la misrad ha menahel ve olai leeishaher achrei beit sefer.

School

Test - Mivchan / **Quiz** - Bochan, chidon
Lesson - Shi'oor / **Notes** - Reshimot
Homework - Shi'hoo'reem / **Assignment** - Matala / **Project** - Proyect
Pencil - Eeparon / **Pen** - Ett / **Ink** - Di'yo / **Eraser** - Mochek
Backpack - Tarmil / teek gav
Book - Sefer / **Folders** - Teek'ee'ya / **Notebook** - Machberet / **Papers** - Dap'eem
Calculator - Machshevon
Glue - Devek / **Scissors** - Misparaiim
Adhesive tape - Tzelotape
Lunchbox - Koofsat ochel / **Lunch** - Aroochat tzhoraiim / **Cafeteria** - Cafetería
Kindergarten - Gan chova / **Pre-school** - Trom chova / **Day care** - Mahon yom
Triangle - Meshulash / **Square** - Ree'boo'aa / **Circle** - Eegool
Crayons - Efronot

Today, we don't have a test but we have a surprise quiz.
Hayom ein-lanu (we don't have) mivchan aval yesh lanu bochan afta'ha.
Are a pen, a pencil, and an eraser included with the school supplies?
Haiim et, iparon, ve mochek klooliim ba aspakat (supplies) beit ha sefer?
I think my notebook and calculator are in my backpack.
Ani choshev shae ha machberet ve ha machshevon sheli nimtzaiim ba tarmil sheli.
All my papers are in my folder.
Kol ha dapiim hem ba machberet sheli.
I need glue and scissors for my project.
Ani tzarich devek ve mispariim la proyect sheli.
I need tape and a stapler to fix my book.
Ani tzarich tzelotape ve mehadek kedei letaken et ha sefer sheli.
You have to concentrate in order to take notes.
Ata tzarich leitrakez kedei lirshom reshimot.
The school librarian wants to invite the art and music teacher to the library next week.
Safranit (librarian) beit ha sefer rotza lehazmin et ha mora le omanut ve et mora le musica la sifriya ba shavoa'a haba.
For lunch, your children can purchase food at the cafeteria or they can bring food from home.
Le aroochat ha tzhoraiim ha yeladim shelachem yecholim liknot ochel ba cafeteria o lahavi ochel mei ha bait.
I forgot my lunchbox and crayons at home.
Shachachti et koofsat ha tzehoraiim ve et ha efronot sheli ba bait.
To draw shapes such as a triangle, square, circle, and rectangle is easy.
Kal (easy) letzayer tzoorot kmo (such as) meshulash, reebo'ha, eegool, ve malben.
During the week, my youngest child is at daycare, my middle one is in pre-school, and the oldest is in kindergarten.
Bae mahalach (throughout) ha shavoa'a ha yeled ha tzaiir sheli nimtza ba ma'aon yom, beni ha emtzaii ba gan, ve ha gadol beyoter nimtza ba gan chova.

PROFESSION - MIKTZOA'A

Doctor - Rofei, **(f)** Rofa / **Nurse** - Ach, **(f)** achot
Psychologist - Psicholog, **(f)** Psicholog'eet / **Psychiatrist** - Psichi'ater, **(f)** psichi'atreet
Veterinarian - Veterinar / **(f)** veterinareet
Lawyer - Orech deen, **(f)** orechet deen /prak'leetan, **(f)** prak'leetan'eet
Judge - Shofet / **(f)** shofetet
Pilot - Tayas, **(f)** tayeset / **Flight attendant** - Dayal, **(f)** dayelet
Reporter - Katav, **(f)** katevet / **Journalist** - Eetona'ee, **(f)** eetona'eet
Electrician - Chashmela'ee / **Mechanic** - Mechona'ee
Investigator - Choker, **(f)** chokeret / **Detective** - Balash
Translator - Metarg'em / **(f)** metarg'emet
Producer - Mafeek, **(f)** mafeeka / **Director** - Menahel

What's your profession?
Ma ha miktzoa'a shelcha?
I am going to medical school to study medicine because I want to be a doctor.
Ani olech/olechet lebeit sefer lerefoha ki ani rotzei/rotza leiyot rofei/rofa.
There is a difference between a psychologist and a psychiatrist.
Yesh evdel (difference) ben pischolog ve psychiater.
Most children want to be astronauts, veterinarians, or athletes.
Rov ha yeladiim rotzim liyot astronaut'eem, veterinar'eem, o sporta'eem.
The judge spoke to the lawyer at the court house.
Ha shofet sochei'ach eem ha orech'deen ba beit-ha-mishpat (court house).
The police investigator needs to investigate this case.
Choker ha mishtara tzarich lachkor et ha meekrei (case) ha ze.
Being a detective could be a fun job.
Liyot balash yachol liyot avoda mehana (fun).
The flight attendant and the pilot are on the plane.
Ha dayal ve ha tayas nimtzaheem al ha matos.
I am a certified electrician.
Ani chashmela'ee moos'mach (certified).
The mechanic overcharged me.
Ha mechona'ee lakach mem'en'ee schar (payment) me'al (over) ha mekoobal (usual).
I want to be a journalist.
Ani rotzei/rotza liyot eetona'ee/eetona'eet.
The best translators work at my company.
Meetav (the best/finest) ha metargem'eem ovdiim ba chevra sheli.
Are you a photographer?
Ha'iim ata/att tzalam/tzalemet?
The author wants to find a ghostwriter to write his book.
Ha sofer rotzei limtzo sofer refa'hiim shei ichtov et ha sefer shelo.
I want to find the directors of the company.
Ani rotzei/rotza limtzo et menahel ha chevra.

Artist (performer) - Oman / omaniit
Artist (draws paints picture) - Tzayar / tzayariit
Author - Sofer / **(f)** soferet
Painter - Tzabai / **(f)** tzabahit
Dancer - Rakdan / **(f)** rakdaniit
Writer - Katav / **(f)** kataviit
Photographer - Tzalam / **(f)** tzalemet
A cook - Tabach / **(f)** tabachiit / **A chef** - Tabach rashi
Waiter - Meltzar / **(f)** meltzariit
Bartender - Barmen / **(f)** barmeniit
Barber shop - Maspera / **Barber** - Sapar / **(f)** sapariit
Stylist - Meha'tzev / **(f)** meha'tzevet
Maid - Ozeret / **Housekeeper** - Ozeret ba'itt
Caretaker - Metapel / metapelet
Farmer - Eekar
Gardner - Ganan
Mailman - Davar
A guard - Shomer / **(f)** shomeret
A cashier - Kupa'ee / **(f)** kupa'eet

The artist produced this artwork for her catalog.
Ha omaniit efeeka et yetzirot ha omanut ba katalog shela.
The artist drew a sketch.
Ha oman tzi'yer skitza (sketch).
I want to apply as a cook at the restaurant instead of as a waiter.
Ani rotzei lahagish me'omad'oot kee tabach ba misa'adah bimkom ke meltzar.
The gardener can only come on weekdays.
Ha ganan yachol lavo rak bae yamei-chol (weekdays).
I have to go to the barbershop now.
Ani tzarich/tzreicha lalechet la maspera achshav.
Being a bartender isn't an easy job.
Liyot bamen/barmeniit zot lo avoda kala.
Why do we need another maid?
Lama anu tzreichim ozeret acheret?
I want to file a complaint against the mailman.
Ani rotze/rotzei lahagish tloona (complaint) neg'ed ha do'ar.
I am a part-time artist.
Ani tzayar bemiisra (shift) chelkiit (part-time).
She was a dancer at the play.
Hee hayta rakdaniit ba atzaga.
You need to contact the insurance company if you want to find another caretaker.
Ata tzariich litzor kesher iim chevrat ha bitoach eem ata rotzei limtzo metapelet chadasha.
The farmer can sell us ripened tomatoes today.
Ha eekar yachol limkor lanu (to us) agvanyot bshelot (ripened).

BUSINESS - ASAKIIM

A business - Essek, (p) asakiim / **Company** - Chevra / **Factory** - Mifhal, beit charoshet
A professional - Miktzohee
Position - Misra / **Work, job** - Avoda / **Employee** - Oved / **(f)** ovedet
Owner - Bahal ha esek, ba'al ha chevra
Management - An'hala / **Manager** - Menahel, **(f)** menahelet
Secretary - Maskira
An interview - Re'ayon / **Resumé** - Korot hachayiim
Presentation - Matzeg'et
Specialist - Mumchei
To hire - Lehaskir / **To fire** - Lefater
Pay check - Maskoret / **Income** - Hachnasa / **Salary** - Sachar
Insurance - Bitooach / **Benefits** - Hatavot
Trimester - Shlish / **Budget** - Taktziv
Net - Neto / **Gross** - Bruto
To retire - Lifrosh / **Pension** - Pensiya, gimlona'oot

I need a job.
Ani tzariich avoda.
She is the secretary of the company.
Hee ha mazkira shel ha chevra.
The manager needs to hire another employee.
Ha menahel tzarich leha'asiik oved acher.
I am lucky because I have an interview for a cashier position today.
Lemazali (it's my good luck) yesh li rea'ayon bishvil misrat ha koopa'iit hayom.
How much is the salary and does it include benefits?
Ma hu ha sachar ve haiim hu kolel (include) hatavot?
Management has your resumé and they need to show it to the owner of the company.
La an'hala yesh et korot ha chaiim shelcha/shelach ve hem tzrichim lehar'ott et zei le ba'al ha chevra.
I am at work at the factory now.
Ani ba avoda ba beit ha charoshet hayom.
In business, you should be professional.
Be asakiim ata tzarich lei'yot miktzohee.
Is the presentation ready?
Haiim ha matzeg'et moochana (ready)?
The first trimester is part of the annual budget.
Ha shlish ha rishon hu chelek (part) mei hataktziiv ha shnati (annual).
I have to see the net and gross profits of the business.
Ani tzarich lir'ott et ha revach ha neto ve ha bruto shel ha esek.
I want to retire already.
Ani rotzei/rotza kvar (already) lifrosh.

Client - Lakohach / **(f)** lekocha
Broker - Metavech / metavechet
Salesperson - Zaban, **(f)** zabaniit / mocher, **(f)** mocheret
Realtor - Metavech dir'ot, **(f)** metavachat dir'ot / Nadlan, **(f)** nadlaniit
Real Estate Market - Shook ha nadlan
A purchase - Rechisha / **A lease -** Chozei sechiroot / **To lease -** Lehaskir
To invest - Lehashkiya / **Investment -** Hashkaha / **Investor -** Ha mashkiya
Landlord - Ba'al ha bait, **(f)** ba'alat ha bait / **Tenant -** Dayar, **(f)** dayeret
Economy - Kalkala
Mortgage - Mashkanta / **Interest rate -** Ribiit / **A loan -** Alva'ha
Commission - Am'la / **Percent -** Achooz
A sale - Mechira / **Profit -** Revach
Value - Erech
The demand - Ha bikoosh / **The supply -** Ha hai'tzaa
A contract - Chozae / **Terms -** Tna'iim / **Signature -** Chatima / **Initials -** Rashei-tevot
Stock - Mena'ya, **(p)** mena'yot / **Stock broker -** Metavech mena'yot
Advertisement - Pirsoom, pirsomet / **Ads -** Moda'hott / **To advertise -** Lefarsem

I can earn a huge profit from stocks.
Ani yachol lahasot revach atzoom (huge) mei ha menayot.
The demand in the real estate market depends on the country's economy.
Ha bikoosh ba shook ha nadlan talooy (depends) ba kalkalat ha medina.
If you want to sell your home, I can recommend a very good realtor.
Iim ata rotzei limkor et ha bait shelcha, ani yachol lahamlitz hal metavech tov me'od.
The investor wants to invest in this shopping center because of its good potential.
Ha mashkiya rotzei lehashkiya bemerkaz ha kniyot hazei mikevan shei yesh potensyal gadol.
The value of the property increased by twenty percent.
Ha erech shel ha neches ala (increased) bei esreem achooz.
How much is the commission on the sale?
Ma hee ha amla shel ha mechira?
The client wants to lease instead of purchasing the property.
Ha lakohach rotzei lehaskiir bimkom lirkosh et ha neches.
What are the terms of the purchase?
Ma hem ha tnaiim shel ha rechisha?
I can negotiate a better interest rate.
Ani yachol lenahel masa-hu-matan (negotiation) al ribit tova yoter.
I need a small loan in order to pay my mortgage this month.
Ani tzarich/tzreicha al'va'ha ktana kedi leshalem et ha mashkanta sheli kol chodesh
I need a signature and initials on the contract.
Ani tzarich/tzreicha chatiima ve et rashei ha tevot al ha chozae.
My position in the company is marketing and I am responsible for advertising and ads.
Tafkidi ba chevra hazot hoo shivook (marketing) ve achrayoot al hapirsoom ve moda'hott.

Business

Money - Kesef, mamon / **Currency** - Matbe'a
Cash - Mezuman / **Coins** - Matbehot
Change (change for a bill) - Odef
Credit - Ashrai
Tax - Mas / **(p)** missiim
Price - Mechir
Invoice - Cheshboniit
Inventory - Mlayee
Merchandise - Secho'ra
A refund - Echzer kaspi
Product - Mutzar
Produced - Meyutzar
Retail - Kim'ona'oot
Wholesale - Sitoonoot
Imports - Yevo'ha / **Exports** - Yetzu'ha
To ship - Lishloach
Shipment - Hovala

Don't forget to bring cash with you.
Al tishkach lehavi mezuman itcha.
Do you have change for a 100 shekel bill?
Yesh lecha/lach odef leshtar shel me'aa shekel?
I don't have a credit card.
Ein li kartis ashrai.
The salesperson told me there is no refund.
Ha mocher amar shae-ein efsharoot (possibility) le echzer.
This product is produced in Italy.
Ha mutzar hazei hu totzeret italya.
I work in the export/import business.
Ani oved ba tchoom (line of expertise) shel yetzoo ve yevoo.
Let me check my inventory.
Ten-li (allow me) livdok et ha mlayee sheli.
This product is insured.
Ha mutzar hazei mevootach.
This invoice contains a mistake.
Ba cheshbonoot hazot yesh tahoot.
What is the wholesale and retail value of this shipment?
Ma hu ha erech ha sitoni ve ha kimona'ee shel ha mishloach hazei?
You don't have enough money to purchase the merchandise.
Ein lecha/lach maspiik (enough) kesef lirchosh et ha schora.
How much does the shipping cost and is it in foreign currency?
Kama olei ha mishloach ve ha'iim hu be matbeiha zaar (foreign)?
There is a tax exemption on this income.
Yesh ptor (exemption) mei mas ha achnasa ha zae.

SPORTS - SPORTS

Basketball - Kadoor sal / **Soccer -** Kadoor reg'el
Game - Mischak / **Stadium -** Iitz'tadyon / **Ball -** Kadoor
Player - Sachkan / **(f)** sachkaniit
To jump - Likfotz / **To throw -** Lizrok / **To kick -** Livhot / **To catch -** Litfos
Coach - Mae'amen / **(f)** mae'amenet / **Referee -** Shofet
Competition - Tacharoot
Team - Nivcheret, kvootza / **Teammate -** Chaver ba kvootza
National team - Kvootza lehoomiit
Opponent - Mitnag'ed
Half time - Chatzi ha zman / **Finals -** Ha gmar
Scores - Totzahott
The goal - Ha shahar / **A goal -** Matara
To lose - Lehafsiid / **A Defeat -** Efsed / **To win -** Lenatzeiach / **A victory -** Nitzachon
The looser - Ha mafseed / **The winner -** Ha mena'tzei'ach
Fans - Meharitziim
Field - Migrash
Helmet - Casda / **A whistle -** Mashrokeet
Basket - Sal
Penalty - Onesh

I like to watch basketball games.
Ani neiheinei (enjoy) litzpot bae mischak ha kadoor sal.
Soccer is my favorite sport.
Kadoor reg'el ze ha sport ha hahoov alai beyoter (the most).
To play basketball, you need to be good at throwing and jumping.
Kedei lesachek kadoor sal ata tzarich lizrok ve likfotz ai'tev.
The national team has a lot of fans.
Ba nivcheret yesh arbei ma'aritziim.
My teammate can't find his helmet.
Chaver ha kvootza eino yachol limtzo et ha casda shelo.
The coach and the team were on the field during half-time.
Ha me'amen ve ha nivcheret hayu al ha migrash bae machatzit ha zman.
The coach needs to bring his team today to meet the new referee.
Ha me'amen tzarich lahavi et ha kvootza shelo hayom lifgosh et ha shofet ha chadash.
Our opponents went home after their defeat.
Ha yeriviim shelanu chazru habayta achrei ha tvoosa (defeat) shelahem.
I have tickets to a soccer game at the stadium.
Yesh li kartisiim la mischak kadoor-reg'el ba itzadyon.
The player received a penalty for kicking the ball in the wrong goal.
Ha sachkan kibel "pendal" al be'itat ha kadoor la sha'ar ha lo-nachon (wrong).
Not every person likes sports.
Lo kol adam ohev sport.

Athlete - Atlet / **(f)** atlet'iit
Olympics - Olimpi'yada / **World cup** - Sha'ar olami / gavi'a olami
Bicycle - Ofanaiim / **Cyclist** - Rochev ofaniim / **Swimming** - Schee'ya
Wrestling - Ivook / **Boxing** - Iigroof / **Martial arts** - Omanoo'yot ha lechima
Championship - Alifoot / **Award** - Prass / **Tournament** - Tacharoot
Horse racing - Merootz soosiim / **Racing** - Merootz
Exercise - Hita'amloot, pei'loot goofaneet / **Fitness** - Ko'sheir goofani
Gym - Cheder ko'sheir, chadar hita'mloot
Captain - Captain, rosh ha kvootza / **Judge** - Shofet, **(f)** shofetet
A match - Mischak / **Rules** - Chookiim / **Track** - Maslool
Trainer - Me'amen / **(f)** me'amenet
Pool (billiards) - Bil'yard / **Pool** (swimming pool) - Breicha

Today are the finals for the Olympic Games.
Hayom, hoo yom hagmar shel mischakei ha olympiyada.
Let's see who wins the World Cup.
Bo'hoo nerei mi yenatzei'ach begaviya ha olam.
I want to compete in the cycling championship.
Ani rotzei/rotza lehitcharot bei-tacharoot ha ofanaiim.
I am an athlete so I must stay in shape.
Ani atlet/atlet'iit lachen ani tzariich/tzreicha lee'hyott be kosheir.
After my boxing lesson, I want to go and swim in the pool.
Achrei shioor ha igroof sheli, ani rotze/rotza lischot ba breicha.
He will receive an award because he is the winner of the martial-arts tournament.
Hoo yekabel et ha prass ki hoo zacha (scored) bei tacharoot shel omaniyot ha lechima.
The wrestling captain must teach his team the rules of the game.
Rosh kvootza ha ivook chayav leleamed et ha nivcheret et klaleyi ha mischak.
At the horse-racing competition, the judge couldn't announce the score.
Ba tacharoot ha soos'eem ha shofet lo yachol haya leho'diya et ha totza'ot.
There is a bicycle race at the park today.
Yesh tacharoot ofaniim hayom ba park.
This fitness program is expensive.
Tochnit ha kosheir hazot hee yekara.
It's healthy to go to the gym every day.
Ze bari (healthy) lalechet la chadar ko'sheir kol yom.
Weightlifting is good exercise.
Haramat mishkolot zo pehiloot gofaniit tova.
I want to run on the track today.
Ani rotzei/rotza larootz ba maslool hayom.
I like to win in billiards.
Ani nei'henei lenatzeiach bae bil'yard.
Ice skating is much easier than it seems.
Gleesha al keirach kala yoter mi ma shae ze nira'a.

OUTDOOR ACTIVITIES - PEI'LOOT CHOOTZ

Hiking - Tiyool ragl'ee
Hiking trail - Shviil halicha
Pocket knife - O'lar
Compass - Matzpen
Camping - Machnahoot / **A camp -** Machanei
Campground - Atar machnahoot
RV - Caravan
Tent - O'hel
Campfire - Medura / **Matches -** Gafrooriim / **Lighter -** Matzit
Coal - Pecham
Flame - Lehava
The smoke - Ha a'ashan
Fishing - Da'eeg / **To fish -** Ladoog
Fishing pole - Chaka / **Fishing line -** Choot da'eeg
Hook - Keres / **A float -** Matz'of / **A weight -** Mishkolet / **Bait -** Pita'yonn
Fishing net - Reseht
To hunt - Latzood
Rifle - Rovei

I enjoy hiking on the trail, with my compass and my pocketknife.
Ani neh'enei letayel bashvil eem ha matzpen ve ha olar sheli.
Don't forget the water bottle in your backpack.
Al tishkach lehavi et bakbook (bottle) hamaiim ba tarmil shelcha.
There aren't any tents at the campground.
Ein o'hal'eem ba machanei.
I want to sleep in an RV instead of a tent.
Ani rotzei/rotza lishon ba caravan bimkom ba o'hel.
We can use a lighter to start a campfire.
Anu yecholim lehishtamesh ba matzit kedei lahadlik et ha medura.
We need coal and matches for the trip.
Anu tzreichim pecham ve gafrooriim bishvil tiyool.
Put out the fire because the flames are very high and there is a lot of smoke.
Techabei et ha esh ki ha lehavot me'od gvo'hott ve yesh arbei a'ashan.
There is fog outside and the temperature is below freezing.
Yesh arafel bachootz ve mezeg-ha-aviir (temperature) mitachat (below) la keepa'on.
Where is the fishing store? I need to buy hooks, fishing line, bait, and a net.
Eichan chanoot ha da'eeg? Ani tzarich liknot krasiim, choot da'iig, pita'yon, ve reshet.
You can't bring your fishing pole or your hunting rifle to the campground of the State Park because there is a sign there which says, "No fishing and no hunting."
Ata lo yachol lehavi et ha chaka ve et ha rovei shelcha la gan ha le'oomi ki yesh shelet (a sign) ha omer asoor (forbidden) ladoog ve asoor latzood.

Sailing - Sha'eet
A sail - Mifras
Sailboat - Siraat-mifras / mifrasiit
Rowing - Chateera
A paddle - Mash'ot
Motor - Mano'aa
Canoe - Canoo
Kayak - Kayac
Rock climbing - Tipoos hariim
Horseback riding - Rechivat soosiim
Diver - Tzolel / **(f)** tzolelet
Scuba diving - Tzlila
Skydiving - Tznicha chofsheet
Parachute - Mitznach
Paragliding - Mitznachei rechifa
Hot air balloon - Balon poreiach
Kite - Afifon
Surfing - Glisha
Surf board - Galshan
Ice skating - Gleesha al ha kerach / **Skiing -** Skee

With a broken motor, we need a paddle to row the boat.
Eem mano'aa shavoor anu tzreichim lehishtamesh ba mashot kedei lahasheet et ha seera.
It's important to know how to use a sail before sailing on a sailboat.
Chashoov ladahat eiich lehishtamesh ba mifras lifnei shayeet ba siraat-mifras.
In my opinion, a kayak is much more fun than a canoe.
Leda'ati kayac yoter na'eem mi canoo.
Do I need to bring my scuba certification in order to scuba dive at the coral reef?
Haiim ani tzarich lehavi et mismachei ha tzlila kedei litzlol ba shooneet ha almog'eem?
I have my mask, snorkel, and fins.
Yesh li mashecha, snorkel, ve snapir'eem.
I don't know which is scarier, sky diving or paragliding.
Ani lo yodei'a ma yoter mafcheed (scary), tznicha chofsheet o mitznachei recheefa.
There are several outdoor activities here including rock climbing and horseback riding.
Yesh kan kama pei'looyot chootz kolel tipoos hariim ve rechivat soosiim.
My dream was always to fly in a hot-air balloon.
Ha chalom (dream) sheli tamiid haya lerachef bei balon porei'ach.
We are going skiing on our next vacation.
Ba choofsha haba'a anachnu olcheem leskee.
Where is the surfboard? I want to surf the waves at the beach.
Eifo ha galshan? Ani rotzei liglosh al ha galeem (waves) bechof ha yam.
Ice skating is fun.
Gleesha al kerach ze mehanei (fun) me'od.

ELECTRICAL DEVICES - MACH'SHEE'REY CHASHMAL

Electronic - Electronee
Electricity - Chashmal
Appliance - Machsheer
Oven - Tanoor
Stove - Keerayeem
Microwave - Microgal
Refrigerator - Mekarer / **Freezer -** Makpee
Coffee maker - Mechonat kafae / **Coffee pot-** Kankan kafae
Toaster - Toster
Dishwasher - Madiach keleem
Laundry machine - Mechonat kveesa / **Laundry -** Kveesa
Dryer - Mechonat yeboosh
Fan - Mae'avrer / **Air condition -** Mazgan
Remote control - Shlat rachok
Alarm - Haza'aka
Smoke detector - Galai ashan
Battery - Solela

He needs to pay his electric bill if he wants electricity.
Hoo tzarich leshalem et cheshbon ha chashmal shelo eem hoo rotzae aspakat chashmal.
I want to purchase a few things at the electronic appliance store.
Ani rotzei/rotza liknot kama dvariim ba chanoot le machsherey chashmal.
I can't put plastic utensils in the dishwasher.
Ani lo yachol lahachnis kelei plastic la madiach ha keleem.
I am going to get rid of my microwave and oven because they are not functioning.
Ani niftar (get rid) mi ha mikrogal ve ha tanoor sheli kee hem lo pei'leem.
The refrigerator and freezer aren't cold enough.
Ha mekarer ve ha hakpa'a lo maspeek kaar'eem.
The coffee maker and toaster are in the kitchen.
Mechonat ha kafei ve ha toster hem ba mitbach.
My washing machine and dryer do not function therefore I must wash my laundry at the public laundromat.
Mechonat ha kvisa sheli ve ha meyabesh einam-pei'leem (they don't function) lachen ani tzarich lechabes et ha kveesa sheli ba londromat ha tzibooree (public).
Is this fan new?
Ha'iim ha me'avrer ha zei chadash?
Unfortunately, the new air conditioner unit hasn't been delivered yet.
Letza'ari (unfortunately) yechidat (unit) ha mazgan ha chadasha terem nimsera (delivered).
Is that annoying sound the alarm clock or the fire alarm?
Haiim ha rahash (noise) ha ma'atzben hazei hoo min ha shao'n ha me'orer o azakat esh.
The smoke detector needs new batteries.
Gala'yee ha a'shan zakook le solelot chadashot.

Lamp - Menora / **Light bulb** - Noora
Stereo - Stereo
A (wall) clock - Orlog'een / **A watch** - Sha'on
Vacuum cleaner - Sho'ev avak
Phone - Teléfon / **Text message** - Hoda'at mesiron /**Voice message** - Hoda'a-koleet
Camera - Matzlema
Flashlight - Panas / **Light** - Orr
Furnace - Kivshan / **Heater** - Ha'meseek
Cord - Cabel / **Charger** - Mat'enn
Outlet - Sheka'a
Headsets - Oz'niyot
Door bell - Pa'amon ha delet
Lawn mower - Mekasei'ach de'shaei

The clock is hanging on the wall.
Ha sha'on taloo'yee (hanging) al a keer.
The cordless stereo is on the table.
Ha stereo ha al-choot'ee (cordless) al ha shoolchan.
I still have a home telephone.
Ada'een yesh li telephon beiti.
I need to buy a lamp and a vacuum cleaner today.
Ani tzarich/tzreicha liknot menora ve sho'ev avak ayom.
In the past, cameras were more common. Today, everyone can use their phones to take pictures.
Ba'avar (in the past) ha matzlemot hayu yoter (more) nefotzot (common). Ayom koolam mishtamshim ba telephon'eem shelahem kedei letzalem.
You can leave me a voice message or send me a text message.
Ata yachol lehasheer li hodaa'a koleet o lishloach hoda'at mesiron.
The lights don't function when there is a blackout therefore I must rely on my flashlight.
Ha orot einam metafkedeem ke'shei yesh afsakat chashmal ve lachen ani chayav/chayevet leestamech (to rely) ba panas sheli.
I can't hear the doorbell.
Ani lo yachol/yachola lishmoa'a et pa'amon ha delet.
There is a higher risk of causing a house fire from an electric heater than a furnace.
Yesh sikoon (risk) gavo'a (higher) yoter (more) ligrom sreifat ba'it beshimoosh (with the use of) meseek chashmali ma'asher ha kivshan.
I need to connect the cord to the outlet.
Ani tzarich/tzreicha lechaber et ha cabel la sheka'a.
His lawnmower is very noisy.
Mekasachat ha deshaei shelo mara'aeesh (noisy) me'od.
Why is my headset on the floor?
Mado'a ha oz'ni'yot sheli al ha ritzpa (floor)?

TOOLS - KLEI AVODA

Toolbox - Argaz kel'eem
Carpenter - Nagar
Hammer - Patt'eesh
Saw - Mas'or / **Axe -** Garzen
A drill - Makdecha / **To drill -** Lik'doe'ach
Nail - Masmer / **A screw -** Bo'reg
Screwdriver - Mavreg / **A wrench -** Maftei'ach brag'eem / **Pliers -** Melka'cha'yeem
Paint brush - Mivreshet / **To paint -** Litzboa'a / **The paint -** Tzeva
Ladder - Soo'lam
Rope - Chevel / **String -** Choot
A scale - Mozna'yeem / **Measuring tape -** Seret medida
Machine - Mechona
A lock - Mano'ol / **Locked -** Nao'ol / **To lock -** Lino'ol
Equipment - Tzi'yood
Metal - Matechet / **Steel -** Plada / **Iron -** Barzel
Broom - Mata'tei / **Dust pan -** Ya'eh
Mop - Magav
Bucket - Dl'ee / **Sponge -** Sfog
Shovel - Ett / **A trowel -** Kaaf chafeera

The carpenter needs nails, a hammer, a saw, and a drill.
Ha nagar zakook le masmer'eem, patish, masor, ve makdecha.
The string is very long. Where are the scissors?
Ha choot me'od aroch (long). Eifo ha mispara'eem?
The screwdriver is in the toolbox.
Ha mavreg nimtza ba argaz kel'eem.
This tool can cut through metal.
Ha kl'ee ha zei yachol lachatoch matechet.
The ladder is next to the tools.
Ha soo'lam leyad ha kel'eem.
I must buy a brush to paint the walls.
Alai liknot mivreshet litzbo'a et ha kirot.
The paint bucket is empty.
Dl'ee ha tzeva reik (empty).
It's better to tie the shovel with a rope in my pick up truck.
A'dif likshor et ett ha chafira bei chevel ba tender sheli.
How can I fix this machine?
Keitzad ochal letaken et ha mechona ha zot?
The broom and dust pan are with the rest of my cleaning equipment.
Ha mata'tei ve ha ya'eh nimtza'eem bei-shei'ar (with the rest) ha tziyood (equipment) sheli.
Where did you put the mop and the bucket?
Eifo samta et ha magav ve ha dl'ee?

CAR - OTO / RECHEV / MECHONEET

Engine - Mano'a
Ignition - Hatzata
Steering wheel - Hei'gae
Automatic - Automati
Manual - Yadani
Gear shift - Heeloochim
Seat - Moshav
Seat belt - Chagorat beetachon
Airbag - Kareet aviir
Brakes - Balameem
Hand brake - Balam yadani
Baby seat - Moshav la tinokot / kee'say la tinok
Driver seat - Moshav ha na'hagg
Passenger seat - Moshav ha noseia'a
Front seat - Moshav kidmee
Back seat - Moshav achoree
Car passenger - Nosei'a ha rechev
Warning light - Noorat azhara
Horn (of the car) - Tzoofar
Button - Kaftor

When driving, both hands must be on the steering wheel.
Ke shae nohag'eem shtey (both) ha yadaiim chayvoot liyot al ha hei'gae.
I must take my car to my mechanic because there is a problem with the ignition.
Alai lakachat et ha mechonit sheli la mechona'ee kee yesh baa'aya (problem) eem ha atzata.
What happened to the engine?
Ma kara la mano'a?
The seat is missing a seat belt.
Bamoshav chasera (missing) chagorat bitachon.
I prefer a gear shift instead of an automatic car.
Ani mahadeef heeloocheem bimkom oto otomatee.
The brakes are new in this vehicle
Ha balameem hem chadasheem ba rechev ha zei.
This vehicle doesn't have a handbreak.
Larechev hazei ein balam yadani.
There is an airbag on both the driver side and the passenger side.
Yesh kareet avir gam betzad ha nahag ve gam betzad ha noseia'a.
The baby seat is in the back seat.
Kee'say ha tinok nimtza ba moshav ha achoree.
The warning light button is located next to the stirring wheel.
Noorat ha azhara nimtzet (located) leyad ha hei'gae.

Windshield - Shmasha kidmeet
Windshield wiper - Magav
Windshield fluid - Nozel shmashot
Rear view mirror - Re'ee achoree / mar'a achoreet
Side mirror - Re'ee tzdad'ee / mar'a tzdad'eet
Door handle - Yad'eet ha delet
Spare tire - Tzameeg chaloofee
Trunk - Taa mita'an
Hood (of the vehicle) **-** Michsei ma'no'aa
Alarm - Aza'aka
Window - Chalon
Drive license - Rishayon ne'hee'ga
License plate - Tzlocheet
Gas - Delek
Low fuel - Delek namooch
Flat tire - Teker
Crowbar - Hamot harama
A (car) jack - Mag'bee'ha
Wrench - Maftei'ach brag'eem

The windshield and all four of my car windows are cracked.
Ha shmasha ha kidmeet ve kol arba'at ha chalonot ba rechev sheli sdook'eem (cracked).
I want to clean my rear-view mirror and my side mirrors.
Ani rotzei/rotza lenakot et re'hee ha achoree sheli ve et mar'ott ha tzadadee'yot.
My car doesn't have an alarm.
Een aza'aka ba mechonit sheli.
Does this car have a spare tire in the trunk?
Ha'iim yesh tzamig chaloofee (spare) ba taa ha mita'an sheli?
Please, close the car door.
Bevakasha, sgor/sigrei et delet ha mechoneet.
Where is the nearest gas station?
Eifo tachanat ha delek ha krova-beyoter (the nearest)?
The windshield wipers are new.
Megavei ha shmasha ha kidmyeem hem chadashiim.
The door handle on the driver's side doesn't function.
Yadeet ha delet bae tzad ha nahag lo po'elet.
Your license plate has expired.
Loocheet ha resho'ee shelcha kvar lo betokef.
I want to renew my driving license today.
Hayom ani rotzei/rotza lechadesh et rishayon ha ne'hee'ga sheli.
Are the car doors locked?
Haiim dlat'oot ha oto ne'ool'ott?

NATURE - TE'VAA

A plant - Tzemach
Forest - Ya'ar
Tree - Etz / **Wood -** Etz
Trunk - Gaeza / **Branch -** Anaf / **Leaf -** Alaei / **Root -** Shoresh
Flower - Peirach
Petal - A'alei ha koteret
Blossom - Preecha
Stem - Guivo'l / **Seed -** Zera, gar'een
Rose - Vered
Nectar - Tzoof / **Pollen -** Avkaneem
Vegetation - Tzimchiya
Bush - See'ach
Grass - Deshaei
Rain forest - Ya'ar geshem / **Tropical -** Tropi / **Palm tree -** Etz dekel
Season - Ona / **Spring -** Aviv / **Summer -** Ka'yeetz / **Winter -** Choref / **Autumn -** Stav

I want to collect a few leaves during the fall.
Ani rotze lehesof kama (a few) alim bae mahalach (during/throughout) ha shalechet (fall).
There aren't any plants in the desert during this season.
Ein tzmachim ba midbar bezman (during the time) ha ona hazot.
The trees need rain.
Ha etziim zkookim legeshem.
The trunk, the branches, and the roots are all parts of the tree.
Ha geza, ha anafeem, ve ha shorashim em chelkyee ha etz.
My rose bushes are beautiful.
Seechei ha vradim sheli yafeifi'eem.
Where can I plant the seeds?
Eichan oochal lizroa'a et ha zra'eem?
I must trim the grass and vegetation in my garden.
Alai lekatzetz et ha deshaei ve ha tzimchi'ya ba guina sheli.
The rain forest is a nature preserve.
Ya'aar ha geshem hoo shmorat (preserve) teva.
Palm trees can only grow in a tropical climate.
Atzei ha dekel yecholim litzmoach rak bae aklim (climate) tropi.
I am allergic to pollen.
Yesh li alerguia la avkaneem/Ani alergui la avkaneem.
The orchid needs to bloom because I want to see its beautiful petals.
Ha sachlav tzarich lifroach ki ani rotzei/rotza lir'ott et alei ha koteret ha yafiim shelo.
Is the nectar from the flower sweet?
Ha'iim tzoof ha perach matok (sweet)?
Be careful because the plant stem can break very easily.
Heeza'her ki giv'ol ha tzemach yachol lehishaver me'od baekaloot (easily).

Lake - Agam
Sea - Yam
Ocean - Okyan'oos
Waterfall - Mapal ma'eem
River - Nahar / **Canal -** Te'a'la / **Swamp -** Bitza
Mountain - Haar / **Hill -** G'eeva'a / **Cliff -** Tzook / **The peak -** Ha pisga
Rainbow - Keshet
Cloud - Anan
Lightning - Barak / **Thunder -** Ra'am
Rain - Geshem / **Snow -** Sheleg
Ice - Keirach / **Hail -** Barad
Fog - A'arafel
Wind - Roo'ach / **Air -** Aveer
Dawn - Shachar / **Dew -** Tal
Sunset - Shkee'ya / **Sunrise -** Zricha

There is a rainbow above the waterfall.
Yesh keshet me'al la mapal.
The ocean is bigger than the sea.
Ha okyan'oos gadol mei ha yam.
From the mountain, I can see the river.
Min ha haar ani yachol lir'ot et ha nahar.
Today we hope to see snow.
Hayom anu mekavim (we hope) lir'ot sheleg.
There aren't any clouds in the sky.
Ein ananeem ba shamaiim.
I see the lightning from my window.
Ani ro'ei brak'eem mi ha chalon sheli.
I can hear the thunder from outside.
Ani yachol lishmo'a re'am'eem ba chootz.
I want to see the sunset from the hill.
Ani rotzei lir'ot et ha shki'ya mi ha giv'a.
The lake has a shallow part and a deep part.
Ba agam yesh chelek ra'dude ve chelek a'amok.
I don't like the wind.
Ani lo ohev/ohevet et ha roo'ach.
The air on the mountain is very clear.
Ha avir ba haar me'od tzalool (clear).
Every dawn, there is dew on the leaves of my plants.
Bechol a'loott-ha (rise of) shachar yesh tal al alei ha tzmacheem sheli.
Is this ice or hail?
Haiim ze kerach o barad.
I can see the volcano.
Ani yachol/yechola lir'ott et haar ha ga'ash.

Nature

Sky - Shamaiim
World - Olam / **Earth** - Kadoor ha aretz
Sun - Shemesh / **Moon** - Yarei'ach / **Crescent** - Sahar / **Full moon** - Levana
Star - Kochav / **Planet** - Kochav lechet
Fire - Esh / **Heat** - Cho'm / **Humidity** - Lachoot
Agriculture - Chaklahoot / **Field** - Sa'deh
Weeds - Asaveem
Rock - Sel'a / **Stone** - Ev'en
Ground / soil - Adama
Island - Ee'ee
Cave - Maea'ara
Public park - Gan tziboori / **National park** - Gan le'oo'mee
Sea shore - Chof ha yam / **Seashell** - Tzdafa
Horizon - Ofek
Ray - Keren
Dry - Yavesh / **Wet** - Ratoov
Deep - A'amok / **Shallow** - Ra'dude
A stick - Makel
Dust - Avak

The moon and the stars are beautiful in the night sky.
Ha yarei'ach ve ha kochav'eem yafiim bei shmei ha laila.
The earth is a planet.
Kadoor ha aretz nechshav le kochav lechet.
The heat today is unbearable.
Ha chom hayom bilti-nisbal (unbearable).
At the beach there is fresh air.
Bae chof ha yam yesh aviir-tzach (*tzach* - "fresh", however *tari* is "fresh" relating to foods).
I want to sail to the island to see the sunrise.
Ani rotzei/rotza lahafleeg la e'ee lir'ot et ha zreecha.
Parts of the cave are dry and other parts are wet.
Chelekei ha me'ara yavesh'eem ve chelak'eem acherim retoov'eem.
We live in a beautiful world.
Anu chaeem bae olam yefei'fei.
There is dust from the fire in the park.
Yesh avak mae ha esh ba gan.
I want to collect seashells from the seashore.
Ani rotze/rotza le'esof tzdafim al chof ha yam.
There are too many stones in the soil so it's impossible to use this area as a field for agricultural purposes.
Yesh yoter midai avan'eem ba adama ve lachen ze bilti-efshari (impossible) lehishtamesh ba ezor (area) azei kee sa'deh lematarot (purposes) chakla'ee'yot.
Why are there so many weeds growing by the swamp?
Madoo'a yesh kol kach harbei asaveem shei tzomchim al yad ha bitza?

ANIMALS - CHAYOT / BA'ALEI CHA'EEM

Animal - Chaya / ba'al chay
Pet - Chayot machmad
Mammals - Yonkeem
Dog - Kelev, **(f)** kalba / **Cat -** Chatool, **(f)** chatoola
Parrot - Tookee
Pigeon - Yona
Pig - Chazir
Sheep - Kivsa / **(m)** keves
Cow - Par'a / **Bull -** Shor
Donkey - Chamor / **Horse -** Soos
Camel - Gamal
Rodent - Mecharsem
Mouse - Achbar / **Rat -** Achbarosh
Rabbit - Shafan, arnev'et (hare) / **Hamster -** Og'er
Duck - Barvaz / **Goose -** Avaz
Turkey - Tarnegol ho'doo / **Chicken -** Tarneg'olet, **(m)** tarnegol / **Poultry -** Of'ott
Squirrel - Sna'ee

I have a dog and two cats.
Yesh li kelev ve shnei chatoolim.
There is a bird on the tree.
Yesh tzipor aa'l ha etz.
I want to go to the zoo to see the animals.
Ani rotzei/rotza lalechet la gan chayot kedey lir'ott et ba'alei ha chay'eem.
My daughter wants a pet horse.
Ha bat sheli rotza soos kee chayat machmad.
A pig, a sheep, a donkey, and a cow are considered farm animals.
Chazir, kivsa, chamor, huu par'a nechshav'eem ke chayot kfar.
I want a hamster as a pet.
Ani rotzei/rotza og'er kee chayat machmad.
A camel is a desert animal.
Gamal hoo chayat midbar.
Can I put ducks, geese, and turkeys inside my coop?
Hayeem ochal laseem barvaz'eem, avaz'eem, ve tarnegol'ayee hodoo ba lool (coop) sheli?
We have rabbits and squirrels in our yard.
Yesh lanoo arnav'ott ve sna'eem ba chatzer (yard) shelanoo.
It's cruel to keep a parrot inside a cage.
Ze achzari (cruel) lahachzeek tookee bei kloov (cage).
There are many pigeons in the city.
Yesh harbei yon'eem ba iir.
Mice and rats are rodents.
Achbar'eem ve achbarosh'eem nechsaveem (considered) le mecharsem'eem.

Bear - Dovv
Tiger - Tigris
Lion - Aryae
Hyena - Tzavo'a
Leopard - Namer / **Panther -** Panter
Cheetah - Bardales
Elephant - Peel
Rhinoceros - Karnaf
Hippopotamus - Hipopotam
Bat - Atalef
Fox - Shooa'al / **Wolf -** Ze'ev
Weasel - Ne'mee'ya
Deer - Tzvi
Monkey - Koff / (f) kofa
Otter - Lootra / kel'ev nahar
Marsupial - Chayat kees

There are a lot of animals in the forest.
Yesh harbei ba'alei cha'eem ba ya'ar.
The most dangerous animal in Africa is not the lion, it's the hippopotamus.
Ha chaya achi mesookenet bae africa hee lo ha aryae ela ha hipopotam.
A wolf is much bigger than a fox.
Ze'ev yoter gadol mi shooa'al
Are there bears in this forest?
Ha'eem yesh doob'eem ba ya'ar ha'zei?
Bats are the only mammals that can fly.
Atalef'eem em ha yonkim ha yechideem shae yecholim la'oof.
It's usually very difficult to see leopards in the wild.
Bederech klal kashei me'od lir'ot namer ba teva.
Cheetahs are common in certain regions of Africa.
Bardales'eem nefotzim bae ezorim (regions) mesooyam'eem (certain) bae africa aval neder'eem (rare) bae ezoreem acherim.
Elephants and rhinoceroses are known as very aggressive animals.
Peel'eem ve karnaf'eem hem yedoo'eem ke chayot tok'pani'yot (aggressive) me'od.
I saw a hyena and a panther at the safari yesterday.
Ra'eetee tzavo'a ve panter ba safari etmol.
The largest member of the cat family is the tiger.
Ha tigris hu echad ha chayot ha gdoleem beyoter bae mishpachat (family) ha chatol'eem.
Deer hunting is forbidden in the national park.
Tza'eed (hunting) tzva'eem asoor ba gan ha le'oomee.
There are many monkeys on the branches of the trees.
Al anfei ha etz'eem yeshnam (there are) kof'eem rab'eem.
An opossum isn't a rat but it's a marsupial just like the kangaroo.
Opasoom hoo lo achbarosh ela hoo chayat kees bidyook (exactly) kmo ha ken'gae'roo.

Animals

Bird - Tzi'porr
Crow - O'rev
Stork - Chaseeda
Vulture - Nesher / **Eagle** - A'eet (However, in Biblical Hebrew "eagle" is *nesher*)
Owl - Yanshoof
Peacock - Tavas
Reptile - Zochel
Turtle - Tzav
Snake - Nachash / **Lizard** - Leta'a / **Crocodile** - Tan'een
Frog - Tzfardei'a
Seal - Kelev yam
Whale - Livyatan / **Dolphin** - Dolfin
Fish - Dagg
Shark - Kareesh
Wing - Kanaf / **Feather** - Notzha
Tail - Zanav
Fur - Parva
Scales - Kaskas'eem
Fins - Snapeer'eem
Horns - Karna'eem
Claws - Tefrei

An eagle and an owl are birds of prey however vultures are scavengers.
A'eet ve yanshoof em off'ott dorseem aval neshar'eem em ochlei-nevelot (scavengers).
Crows are very smart.
Orv'eem me'od chacham'eem (smart).
I want to see the stork migration in Israel.
Ani rotzei/rotza lir'ot et nedidat (migration) ha chaseed'ott bae ees'ra'el.
Don't buy a fur coat!
Al tikn'ei me'il (coat) parva!
Butterflies and peacocks are colorful.
Parpar'eem ve tavas'eem hem tzivonee'yeem (colorful).
Some snakes are poisonous.
Chelek mei ha nachash'eem hem arsee'eem (poisonous).
Is that the sound of a cricket or a frog?
Ha'eem ze kol ha tzar'tzar o ha tzfardei'a.
Lizards, crocodiles, and turtles belong to the reptile family.
Leta'ott, taneen'eem, ve tzaveem shayach'eem-le (belong to) mishpachat ha zochal'eem.
I want to see the fish in the lake.
Ani rotzei lir'ott et ha dagg ba a'gam.
There were a lot of seals basking on the beach last week.
Hayu harbei kalbei yam al ha chof bae shavo'a shae'avar (past).
A whale is not a fish.
Livyatan hoo lo dagg.

Insect - Charak
A cricket - Tzar'tzar
Ant - Nemala **/ Termite -** Term'eet
A fly - Zvoov **/ Mosquito -** Yatoosh **/ Flea -** Barchash **/ Lice -** Keen'eem
Butterfly - Parpar
Worm - Tol'a'att
Beetle - Chiposheet
A roach - Teekan / tjook
Bee - Dvora
Spider - Akaveesh **/ Scorpion -** A'krabb
Snail - Cheelazonn
Invertebrates - Chasrei chool'yot
Shrimps - Chaseelon'eem **/ Clams -** Tzdafoot **/ Crab -** Sartan
Octopus - Tamnoon
Starfish - Kochav yam
Shell - Koon'chee'ya (snail shell), shiryon (turtle shell)

An octopus has eight tentacles.
La tamnoon yesh shmonah zro'ott (tentacles).
A jellyfish is a common dish in Asian culture.
Medusa nechshevet le ma'achal (a dish) nafotz ba tarboot (culture) ha asyaty't.
The museum has a large collection of invertebrate fossils.
La mozei'onn yesh osef (collection) gadol shel chasrei chool'yott meooban'eem (fossils).
I want to buy mosquito spray.
Ani rotzei/rotza liknot tarsees (spray) le yatoosh'eem.
I need antiseptic for my bug bites.
Ani tzarich/tzreicha chitoo'ee (antiseptic) neg'ed akitzoot (bites) ha charak'eem.
I hope there aren't any worms, ants, or flies in the bag of sugar.
Ani mekavei/mekava shae ba sac ha soocar ein tola'eem, nemal'eem, o zvoov'eem.
I have crabs and starfish in my aquarium.
Yesh lee sartan'eem ve kochavei yam ba akvar'yoom (aquarium) sheli.
Certain types of spiders and scorpions can be dangerous.
Soog'eem (types) mesooyam'eem (certain) shel akaveesh'eem ve a'krabb'eem yecholeem lehi'yot mesookaneem.
I need to call the exterminator because there are fleas, roaches, and termites in my house.
Ani tzarich likro la merases (exterminator) mikevan shae yesh harbei barchash'eem, teekan'eem ve termit'eem ba ba'itt sheli.
Bees are very important for the environment.
Ha dvor'ott chashoov'ott me'od la sveeva (environment).
Is there a snail inside the shell?
Ha'eem yesh shablool ba koon'chee'ya (snail shell)?
Beetles are my favorite insects.
Chipoosh'iyot hen ha charakeem ha chav'eev'eem (favorite) alai.

RELIGION, CELEBRATIONS, & CUSTOMS
DA'AT, CHAG'EEM, OO MINHAG'EEM

God - Elo'eem, elo'keem / **Bible** - Tanach
Old Testament - Ha breet ha yeshana / **New Testament** - Ha breet ha chadasha
Adam - Adam / **Eve** - Chava / **Garden of Eden, heaven** - Gan eden
Angels - Mal'ach'eem / **Priest** (in Judaism) - Cohen
Noah - No'ach / **Ark** - Tei'vah
To pray - Lehitpalel / **Prayer** - Tfeela
Blessing - Bracha/ **To bless** - Levarech / **Holy** - Kadosh / **Faith** - Emoona
Moses - Moshe / **Prophet** - Navi / **Messiah** - Mashiach / **Miracle** - Ness
Ten commandments - A'aseret ha dibrot
The five books of Moses - Chameshet sifrei ha torah
Genesis - Beresheet / **Exodus** - Shmot / **Leviticus** - Va'ykra
Numbers - Bameed'bar / **Deuteronomy** - Dvareem

What is your religion?
Ma'ee ha dat shelcha?
Many religions use the bible.
Dat'oot raboot (many) mishtamshot (they use) ba tanach.
We have faith in miracles.
Yesh lanoo emoona bae neseem.
When do I need to say the blessing?
Matai alai lomar et ha bracha?
I must say a prayer for the holiday.
Ani tzarich/tzreicha lomar tfeela la chag.
The angels came from heaven.
Ha malahach'eem heigui'yoo mae hashama'eem.
Aaron, the brother of Moses, was the first priest.
A'aron, acheev shel moshe, haya ha cohen ha rishon (first).
The story of Noah's Ark and the flood is very interesting.
Sipoor (story) teivat noach ve ha mabool (flood) ma'anyen'eem me'od.
Adam and Eve were the first humans and they lived in the Garden of Eden.
Adam ve chava hayu bnei ha adam ha rishon'eem ve hem chayoo be gan eden.
Moses had to climb up on Mount Sinai to receive the Ten Commandments from God.
Moshe ne'elatz letapes al har seen'ayee kedei lekabel et a'aseret ha dibrot.
The Five Books of the Moses are Genesis, Exodus, Leviticus, Numbers, and Deuteronomy.
Chameshet seefrei ha torah hem beresheet, shmot, vaykra, bameedbar, ve dvareem.
Moses was considered as the prophet of all prophets.
Moshe nechshav la navi ha nevi'eem.
My favorite book of the bible is the Book of Prophets.
Sefer ha tanach ha ahoov alai hoo sefer ha nevi'eem.

Jew - Yehoodi / **Judaism** - Yahadoot
Religious - Dat'ee, (f) dat'ee'ya / **Monotheism** - Emoona bea el echad
Synagogue - Beit keneset
Kosher - Kashroot
Passover - Pesach
Menorah - Chanookee'ya
Dreidle - Sevivon
Goblet - Gavi'ya / **Wine** - Ya'een
Circumcision - Brit mila

The Jews worship at the synagogue.
Ha yehoodim mitpal'el'eem ba veit ha keneset
The Bible is a holy book which tells the story of the Jewish nation and includes many miracles.
Ha tanach hoo sefer kadosh shae mesaper et ha sipur shel ha a'am (nation) ha yehoodi ve kolel niseem rabeem.
The three forefathers are Abraham, Isaac, and Jacob.
Sholoshet ha avot hem avraham, itzack, ve ya'akov.
Saturday, Monday, and Thursday we read the biblical portion of the week.
Bae yom shabat, sheni, ve chamishi ano koreem et parashat ha shavoo'a.
In Judaism, they pray three times a day. Morning prayer, afternoon prayer, and evening prayer.
Ba yahadoot mitpalel'eem shalosh pa'am'eem beiyom. Tfilat shacharit, mincha, ve ma'a'riv.
Where is the goblet of wine for Rosh Hashana?
Eichan gaviya ha yaiin (wine) lei rosh hashana?
I want to fast this year on Yom Kippur.
Ani rotzei/rotza latzoom hashana bae yom kippur.
I have a menorah and a dreidel for Hannukah.
Yesh li chanookee'ya ve sevivon le chanukah.
Passover is my favorite holiday.
Pesach ha chag ha ahoov alai.
We welcome the Sabbath by lighting candles.
Ano makbileem et pnei ha shabat be hadlakat ner'ott.
I want to keep kosher.
Ani rotzei/rotza lishmor a'l kashroot.
Where is your yarmulke?
Eichan ha kipa shelcha?
The circumcision is performed on the 8th day after the birth of the child.
Brit ha mila mevootza'at (carried out) ba yom ha shmini le'achar lidato shel ha yeled.
There is a large religious Jewish community in this neighborhood.
Ba shchoona hazoot yesh kehila (community) yehudit dat'eet gdola.
To learn about the Holocaust and the concentration camps is very important.
Chashoov me'od lilmod al ha sho'aa ve al machanot ha reekooz.

Religion, Celebrations, & Customs

The Christian Religion - Ha da'at ha notzreet
Church - Knesi'ya / **Cathedral -** Catedral
Catholic - Catol'ee, **(f)** Catol'eet / **Christian -** Notzree, **(f)** notzree'ya
Christianity - Natzroot / **Catholicism -** Catol'ee'oot
Jesus - Yeshoo / **A cross -** Tzlav
Priest (in Christianity) **-** Comer
Holy - Kadosh / **Holy water -** Ma'eem kdosheem
To sin - Lachto / **A sin -** Chet
Monastery - Minzar
Christmas - Chag hamolad
Christmas eve - Erev chag hamolad
Christmas tree - Etz ha ashoo'ach
New Year - Shana chadasha / **Merry Christmas -** Chag molad same'ach
Easter - Chag ha pascha
Saint - Kadosh, **(f)** kdosha / **Nun -** Nezira / **Chapel -** Beit tfila
Islam - Islam / **Muslim -** Muslemee / **Mohammed -** Mohamed / **Mosque -** Misgad
Hindu - Hindi / **Buddhist -** Bood'eest / **Temple -** Mikdash

The church is open today.
Hayom ha knesi'ya ptoocha.
Christians love to celebrate Christmas.
Ha notzreem ohaveem lachagog et chag ha molad.
Is it possible to turn on the lights on my Christmas tree for Christmas Eve?
Efshar (is it possible) lehadlik et ha orot al etz ha shoo'ach sheli le erev chag ha molad?
Two more weeks until Easter.
Rak od shvo'aim (two weeks) a'd chag ha psacha.
The nuns live in the monastery.
Ha nezir'ott gar'ott ba minzar.
The priest read a psalm from the Bible in front of the congregation.
Ha comer kara mizmor (psalm) mei ha tanach mool (in front of) ha kehila.
I went to pray in the cathedral.
Alachti lehitpalel ba catedrala.
Happy holiday and Happy New Year to all my friends and family.
Chag sameiach ve shana tova le kol ha chaverim sheli ve bnei ha mishpacha.
The priest baptized the baby in the holy water.
Ha comer taval et ha tinok bae ma'yeem kdoshim.
The devil and the demons are from hell.
Ha satan ve ha shed'eem hem mae ha ge'henom
Many schools refuse to teach evolution.
Batei sefer rabim mesarvim lelamed et hitpatchoot-ha-enoshoot (evolution).
The Muslims pray at the mosque.
Ha moslemeem mitpaleleem ba misgad.
In Islam they pray five times a day.
Ba islam mitpalel'eem chamesh pehameem ba yom.

WEDDING AND RELATIONSHIP
NESOO'EEM VE ITYACHASOOT

Wedding - Chatoona / nesoo'eem
Wedding hall - Oo'lam chatoonot
Married - Nasoo'yee
Civil wedding - Chatoona ezrach'eet
Bride - Kala
Groom - Chatan
Ceremony - Tekes
Reception hall - Oolam ha kabala
Chapel - Beit keneset
Engagement - Eerooseem
Engagement ring - Taba'at erooseem
Wedding ring - Taba'at neesoo'eem
Anniversary - Yom ha neesoo'yeem
Honeymoon - Ye'rach dvash
Fiancé - Aroos / **(f)** aroosa
Husband - Ba'al
Wife - Eesha

When is the wedding?
Matai ha chatoona?
We are having the service in the chapel and the reception in the wedding hall.
Anachnu nitpalel bebeit ha kneset ve kabalat ha pan'eem tee'hyae bae oolam ha chatoonot.
Our anniversary is on Valentine's Day.
Yom ha neesooyeen shelanu be yom ha ahava.
This is my engagement ring and this is my wedding ring.
Zot taba'at ha erooseem sheli vzot tabat ha neesooyeem.
They are finally married so now it's time for the honeymoon.
Sof sof (finally) hem nesoo'eem az achshav egui'a-ha-zman (the time has come) la ye'rach ha dvash.
He decided to propose to his girlfriend. She said "yes" and now they are engaged.
Hoo hechelit lehatziya neesooeem la chavera shelo. Hee amra "ken" ve achshav hem mehooras'eem.
He is my fiancé now. Next year he will be my husband.
Hoo ha aroos sheli achshav ve bashana haba'a hoo hee'ee'yae ha bahal sheli.
Three civil weddings are taking place at the courthouse today.
Shalosh chatoonot ezrachee'yot (civil) mitrachshot (taking place) hayom ba veit ha mishpat.
The bride and groom received many presents.
Ha chatan ve ha kala kibloo harbei matan'ot (presents).

Valentine day - Yom ha ahava
Love - Ahava **/ To love -** Le'eh'hov
In love - Mae'o'hav / **(f)** mae'o'hevet
Romantic - Romanti
Darling - Yakiri
A date - Pgeesha
A (romantic) relationship - Yachaseem / zoog'ee'oot (married relationship)
A (non-romantic) relationship - Yachaseem
Boyfriend - Chaver
Girlfriend - Chavera
To hug - Lechabek
A hug - Chibook
To kiss - Lenashek
A kiss - Neshika
Single - Ravak / **(f)** ravaka
Divorced - Garoosh / **(f)** groosha
Widow - Alman / **(f)** almana

I am in love with her (male to female).
Ani mae'hoo'hav ba.
I am in love with him (female to male).
Ani mei'hoo'hevet bo.
I love her (male to female).
Ani ohev ota.
I love him (female to male).
Ani ohevet oto.
I love you (male to female).
Ani ohev otach.
I love you (female to male).
Ani ohevet otcha.
You are very romantic.
Ata me'od romanti.
They have a very good relationship.
Yesh la'hem yachaseem tov'eem.
The husband and wife are happily married.
Ha ba'al ve ha isha hem mehooshar'eem (happy) bae nesoo'eem.
I am single because I divorced my wife.
Ani ravak kee hitgarash'tee mae ishtee.
She is my darling and my love.
Hee yakeera'tee ve ahoova'tee
I want to kiss you and hug you in this picture.
Ani rotzei/rotza lenashek ve lechabek otcha/otach ba tmoona (picture) ha zot.

POLITICS - MEDENI'YOOT

Politics - Medeni'yoot / medeni'yoot polit'eet
Flag - Deg'el
National anthem - Himnon le'oomi
Nation - A'am / o'oma
National - Le'oomi
International - Bein le'oomi
Local - Mekomi
Patriot - Patriot, ohev molad'eto
Symbol - Semel
Peace - Shalom
Treaty - Heskem / breet
State - Medina
Country - Eretz / medina
County - Machoz
Century - Mei'a
Majority - Rov
Local - Mekomi
Campaign - Ma'aracha
Annexation - Seepoach
Plan - Tochn'eet
Strategic - Estrateg'eet
Decision - Hachlata

This is a political movement which is supported by the majority.
Zot tnoo'a polit'eet shae nit'mechet al yade'ee ha rov.
This flag is the national symbol of the country.
Ha deg'el ha ze hoo ha semel ha le'oomi shel ha eretz.
This is all politics.
Kol ze medeni'yoot polit'eet.
There is a difference between state law and local law.
Yesh evdel bein chok ha medina la chok ha mekomi.
He is a patriot of the nation.
Hoo ohev ha ha a'am.
Most countries have a national anthem.
Le rov ha medinot yesh himnon le'oomi.
This is a political campaign to demand independence.
Zot ma'aracha medeen'eet shae doreshet atzma'oot.
The annexation plan was a strategic decision.
Toch'neet ha seep'uuach hayta hachlata estrateg'eet.

Legal - Chook'ee
Law - Chok
Illegal - Lo chook'ee
International law - Chok bein le'oomi
Human rights - Zchoo'yot ha adam
Punishment - Onesh
Torture - Ee'noo'y
Execution (to kill) **-** Hotza'at la oreg
Spy - Meragel
Amnesty - Chaneena
Political asylum - Miklat medeenee
Republic - República
Dictator - Dictator / rodan
Citizen - Ezrach
Resident - Toshav
Immigrant - Mehager
Public - Tziboor'ee **/ Private -** Prat'ee
Racism - Gaz'an'oot
Government - Memshala
Revolution - Mahapaecha
Civilian - Ezrachi **/ A civilian -** Ezrach
Population - Och'loo'siya
Socialism - Socializm
Communism - Comunizm

There were many protests and riots today.
Hayoo arbei mecha'ott ve mehoom'ott hayom.
The civilian population wanted a revolution.
Ha oochloosiya ha ezracheet ratzta mahapaecha.
The politicians want to ask the president to give the captured spy amnesty.
Ha politika'eem rotzeem levakesh mei ha nassee latet chaneena la meragel shae nilkad.
Although he was the brutal dictator of the republic, in private he was a nice person.
Afiloo shae hoo haya rodan achzar'ee (brutal) shel ha republica, bae cha'yav ha prati'eem (private) hay adam nechmad (nice).
In some countries torture and execution is a common form of legitimate punishment.
Bemedinot mesooyamot eenoo'eem ve hotza'a la'horeg hem onash'eem choo'kee'yeem.
This is a violation of human rights and international law.
Zo hafara (violation) shel zchoo'yot ha adam ve ha chok ha bein le'oomi.
Communism and socialism were popular in the 19th century.
Comunizm ve tzocializm hayoo mei'koobaleem ba meiha (century) tsha'esrae'ee.
In which county is this legal?
Bei ezei machoz ze chook'ee?

Politics

President - Nass'ee
Statement - Hatzhara
Presidential - Ness'ee'oot
Vice president - Sgan ha nasee
Defense minister - Sarr ha haganah
Interior minister - Sarr ha pneem
Exterior minister - Sarr ha chootz
Prime minister - Rosh memshala
Election - Becheerot
Poll - Kalpee / kalfee
Election campaign - Maharachat bechirot
Candidate - Mo'oomad
Democracy - Democrat'ya / shilton a'am
Movement - Tnoo'a
Politician - Politika'ee
Politics - Política
To vote - Lahatzbeeya
Majority - Rov
Independence - Atzma'oot
Party - Meeflaga
Veto - Veeto
Impeachment - Hadacha
Convoy - Shayara

They want to appoint him as defense minister.
Em rotzeem lemanot oto ke sarr ha haganah.
Both parties want to veto the impeachment inquiry.
Shtey ha miflagot rotz'ott lehateel veto al chakeerat ha hadacha.
I want to see the presidential convoy.
Ani rotzei/rotza lir'ott et shayeret ha ness'ee'oot.
In some countries other than the United States, they have a prime minister, interior minister, and exterior minister.
Bemedeenot mesooyamot milvad artzot ha brit, yesh rosh memshala, sarr ha pneem, va sarr ha chootz.
I want to meet the president and the vice president.
Ani rotzei lifgosh et ha nassee ve et sgan ha nassee.
I want to go to the election polls to vote for the new candidate.
Ani rotzei/rotza lalechet la kalfee ha bchirot kedey lahatzbeeya la mo'oomad ha chadash.
We support democracy and are against fascism and racism.
Ano tomch'eem (support) ba democratya ve nege'd fash'ism ve gazan'oot.

United Nations - Ha oom
Condemnation - Gui'noo'ee
United States - Artzot ha brit
European Union - Ha eechood erop'ee
Military coup - Maka tzva'iit
Treason - Bgeeda
Fascism - Fash'ism
Resistance - Heetnagdoot
Members - Chaverei
Captured - Tafoos / **To capture -** Leetfoss
Ambassador - Shagreer
Embassy - Shagreer'oot
Consulate - Consool'ya
Biased - Meshoo'chad
Unilateral - Chad tzdadi
Bilateral - Du tzdadi
Resolution - Hachlata
Rebels - Mordeem
Sanctions - Eetzoom'eem

All the members of the resistance were accused of treason and had to ask for political asylum.
Kol chavrei ha heetnagdoot shae hoo'shamoo bebgeeda ne'eltzoo levakesh miklat medinee.
The resolution is biased.
Ha hachlata meshoo'chad.
This was an official condemnation.
Ze haya guinooee reshm'ee (official).
The United Nations is located in New York.
Binyanei-ha (the building of the) oom nimtza'eem bae new york.
I am a United States citizen and a resident of the European Union.
Ani ezrach artzot ha brit ve toshav ha eechood ha eerop'ae'ee.
The ambassador's residence is located near the embassy.
Mekom ha megoor'eem shel ha shagreer hoo samooch (near) la shagreer'oot.
I need the phone number and address of the consulate.
Ani tzarich/tzreicha et mispar ha telefon ve ha ktovet (address) shel ha consool'ya.
Are consular services available today?
Hayeem-nitan (is it possible) lahaseeg she'root'aei (services) ha consul'ee'ya hayom?
The international peace treaty needs to include both sides.
Heskem ha shalom ha bein le'oomi tzarich lichlol et shnei ha tzdadim (sides).
According to the government, the rebels carried out an illegal military coup.
Lef'ee-ha (according to the) memshala, ha mordeem bitz'hoo makat tzva'itt lo chookeet.
They must impose sanctions against that country.
Alei'hem lahateel eetzoom'eem neg'ed ha medina hazot.

MILITARY - TZA'VA

Army - Tza'va / **Armed forces** - Kochot chamoosheem
Navy - Cheil ha yam
Soldier - Chayal
A force - Koach / **Ground forces** - Koach raglee
Base - Bass'ees / **Headquarter** - Mifkada, mataei / **Intelligence** - Modee'een
Ranks - Dargot / **Sergeant** - Samal / **Lieutenant** - Sgan
The general - Aloof / **Commander** - Mefaked / **Colonel** - Aloof mishnei
Chief of Staff - Ramatkal
Enlistment - Gui'yoos
Reserves - Mee'loo'eem
War - Milchama
Terrorism - Ter'or / **Terrorist** - Mechabel / **Insurgency** - Itkomem'oot
Border crossing - Ma'avar ha gvool
Refugee - Pal'eet
Camp - Machanae

I want to enlist in the military.
Ani rotzei/rotza lehitgayes la tza'va.
This base is designated for military aircraft only.
Ha bass'ees hazei mae'yoo'ad (designated) le matos'eem tzva'ee'ym bilvad.
That is the headquarters of the enemy.
Zot mifked'et ha o'yev.
This country has a powerful airforce.
Yesh la medina ha zot cheil aveer chazak (strong).
They need to enlist reserve forces for the war.
Hem tzreicheem legayes kochot meelooyeem la milchama.
Welcome to the border crossing.
Broochim haba'eem le mahavar ha gvool.
Military intelligence relies on important sources of information.
Ha modee'een meestamech al mekorot (sources) meida'a (information) chashooveem.
The chief of staff was the target of a failed assassination attempt.
Ha ramatkal haya ha ya'ad le neesayon eetnakshoot (assassination) koshel (failed).
The sniper killed the highest-ranking lieutenant.
Ha tzalaf harag et ha sgan ha bacheer (high ranking).
The terrorist group claimed responsibility for the car-bomb attack at the refugee camp.
Kvootzat ha ter'or natla (claimed) achrayoot (responsibility) al peegoo'a mechonit ha tofet ba machanaei ha pleet'eem.
It is impossible to defeat terrorism because it's an ideology.
Ze biltee efsharee lenatzeiach ter'or kee zot ideolog'ya.

Air strike - Hatkafa aveer'eet
Air force - Cheil aveer / **Fighter jet -** Matos krav
Military aircraft - Matos tzva'ee
Drone - Mazlat / **Stealth technology -** Technolog'ya chamkan'eet
Tank - Tank / **Submarine -** Tzolelet
Weapon - Neshek
Grenade - Rimon / **Mine -** Mokesh / **Bomb -** Ptzatza / **Explosion -** Heet'potzetz'oot
Sniper - Tzalaf / **Gun -** Ekdach / **Rifle -** Rovei / **Bullet -** Kadoor
Missile - Teel, raketa / **Mortar -** Patzmar
Anti tank missile - Teel neg'ed tank'eem / teel noon'tet
Anti aircraft missile - Teel neg'ed matos'eem / teel noon'mem
Shoulder fire missile - Teel katef
Ammunition - Tachmoshet / **Artillery -** Artillería / **Artillery shell -** Pagaz artiller'ee
Precision missile - Teel medoo'yak
Ballistic missile - Teel balistee
Atomic bomb - Ptzatzat atom / **Nuclear weapon -** Neshek gar'een'ee
Weapon of mass destruction - Neshek le hashmada hamoneet
Chemical weapon - Neshek cheem'ee
Flare system - Ma'arechet ha eetlakchoot
Supply - Haspaka / **Storage -** Ichsoon
Armor - Sheer'yon

The M-16 is a US-made rifle.
Ha M-shesh'esrei hoo rovei mi totzeret (made in) artzot ha brit.
The tank fired artillery shells.
Ha tank yara pagaz'ae'ee artilerya.
Shoulder-fired missiles are extremely dangerous and are hard to defend against.
Teel'ae'ee katef hem me'od mesookan'eem (dangerous) ve kashei lehitgonen negd'am.
The flare system is meant as a defense against anti-aircraft missiles.
Ma'arechet ha itlakchoot mo'edet (meant for) le haganah neg'ed teel'ae'ee noon'mem.
The navy was able to intercept a missile.
Chel hayam heetzlee'ach leyaret teel.
At the terrorist safe-house, guns, bullets, and grenades were found.
Bebeit hamachbo shel ha mechabl'eem neemtze'oo ekdacheem, kadooreem, ve rimoneem.
The coalition forces struck an enemy arms depot.
Kochot ha coalitz'ya pag'oo bemachsan neshek shel ha o'yev.
An intense missile attack was carried out against the supply forces that resulted in many casualties.
Mitkefet teel'eem ha a'aza bootzha'a (carried out) neg'ed kochot ha haspakah shae garma (which resulted in) le neefga'eem (casualties) rabeem.
The terrorist cell fired ballistic missiles at the nuclear facility site.
Choolyat (cell) ha ter'or yarta teel'eem balist'eem la'atar mitkan (facility) ha gar'een.
Atomic bombs and chemical weapons are weapons of mass destruction.
Ptzatz'ott atom ve neshek cheem'ee hem neshek le hashmadah hamoneet.

Military

A target - Ya'ad, matara / **To target** - Lechaven
An attack - Hatkafa / **To attack** - Lehatkeef / **Intense** - A'az
To shoot - Lirot / **Open fire** - Liftoach bae'esh / **Fired** - Ya'ra
Assassination - Chisool, eetnakshoot, retzach / **Assassin** - Rotzei'ach
Enemy - O'yev
Reconnaissance - Siyoor / **To infiltrate** - Lehistanen / **Invasion** - Pleesha
Exchange of fire - Cheelofei esh
A cease fire - Afsakat esh / **Withdrawal** - Neseega
To win - Lena'tze'ach
To surrender - Lehikana'a
Victim - Korban / **Injured** - Pag'oo'a / **Wounded** - Patzoo'a
Deaths - Mavet / **Killed** - Aroogeem / **To kill** - Laharog
Prisoner of war - Aseer milchama
Missing in action - Ne'edar
Act of war - Ma'asae milchama
War crimes - Pishae'ee milchama
Defense - Haganah
Attempt - Neesayon

There is an invasion of ground forces.
Yesh pleesha shel kochot ha yabasha.
The soldier wanted to open fire and shoot at the invading forces.
Ha chayal ratza liftoach bae esh ve lirot bae kochot ha polsheem.
The bomb attack was considered an act of aggression and an act of war.
Ha pee'goo'a nechshav kee ma'asae tokpanoot ve ma'asae milchama.
The reconnaissance drone managed to infiltrate deep within enemy territory.
Mazlat ha see'yor heetzlee'ach lehistanen la o'omek shetach (territory) ha oyev.
The airstrike targeted an ammunition storage site.
Ha tkeefa ha avir'eet koovna neg'ed ha atar le'ichsoon ha tachmoshet.
The mortar attack and exchange of fire caused injuries and deaths on both sides.
Mitkefet ha patzmareem ve cheeloofei ha esh garmoo (lead to) le ptzoo'eem ve mavet beshenei ha tzdadeem.
First, we need to clear the mines.
Kodem-kol (first of all), ano tzrechim lefanot et ha moksheem.
The ceasefire agreement included the release of prisoners of war.
Heskem hafsakat ha esh kalal shichroor aseer'ae'ee ha milchama.
The army made a public statement to announce the withdrawal.
Ha tza'va hetz'heer bae fombee ve ho'odee'aa a'l ha neseega.
There was a huge explosion as a result of the terrorist attack.
Haya pitzootz adir (huge) kee-totza'a (as a result) mi peegoo'a ha mechabl'eem.
The commander of the insurgency was accused of serious war crimes.
Mefaked ha itkomem'oot ho'osham (accused) bae peeshae'ee milchama chamoor'eem.
Several of the submarine sailors were missing in action.
Kama-mae (several of) malachei ha tzolelet ne'edroo ba pae'oola (in the mission).

Basic Grammatical Requirements of the Hebrew Language

*In the Hebrew language, adjectives come after the noun, for example, "sunglasses" / *Mishkafaei* ("glasses") *Shemesh* ("sun"). The same rule also applies for possessive adjectives. For example, "your" / *shelcha;* "my" / *sheli*; and "his" or "hers" / *sehlo* or *shela,* etc., will always follow the noun, and the article "the" / *ha* will always precede the noun. For example:

* "your office" / *Ha* ("the") *misrad* ("office") *shelcha* ("your")

* "his house" / *Ha* ("the") *ba-it* ("house") *shelo* ("his")

* "my place" / *Ha* ("the") *makom* ("place") *sheli* ("my")

*The word *et* in the Hebrew language is a term which is used in order to indicate a definite or direct object, but it depends on how it is used in a sentence. *Et* doesn't directly translate into the English language. So to say "I read," you would say, *Ani Koreh.* To say "I read the book," you would say, *Ani Koreh et ha'sefer.* Because *sefer* ("book") is definite and the direct object, you need both the *et* and the *ha-*. *Et* doesn't have to be followed by a "the" suffix *ha-* ("the") when it is definite without the *ha-*. Such cases include names, so *Ani Koreh Et Shakespeare* would be "I read Shakespeare." *Et* is also very commonly used when describing "that," for example, "I want that" would be *ani rotze et ze.* Just keep in mind that *et* is actually a preposition that is placed before any definite direct object.

*In Hebrew, "because" / *biglal* is always followed by "that" / *shae.* For example, "because I go" is *biglal shae ani olech.*

*In Hebrew, the article *"a"* doesn't exist. For example, in the English language "a book" in Hebrew would translate to *sefer.* Another example is "I want to buy a house" / *ani* ("I") *rotze* ("want") *liknot* ("to buy") *beit* ("house").

*In the English language, first person verbs usually begin with "I am" and end with *-ing*. However, in Hebrew there is no *-ing*, and there is no "am." There is just "I," *ani.* So "I am going" is *"Ani olech."*

*Also, in Hebrew, "you're" is *ata.* There is no "are"; there is only "you," *ata.* Though there is "are you," *ha'iim ata.*

*In Hebrew grammar, gender is always used. In Hebrew, every noun is either masculine or feminine and sometimes both. In this program, whenever you encounter (m.), it will signify "masculine," and (f.) will signify "feminine."

*In Hebrew, in relation to compound words, the article precedes the second word.
"Where is **the** train station?" / *eifo tachanat* **ha** *rakevet?*

*In Hebrew regarding a statement with the definite article of a noun, the article precedes the adjective as well.
For example:
"where is **the** public transportation?" / *eifo* **ha** *tachbura* **ha** *tziburit?*

*In hebrew to signify "and" we use *ve* or *oo*. Any word beginning with *b*, *v*, *m*, *p*, or *f* prior to them *ve* / "and" will become *oo*.
Gan **oo** *vait* / "garden **and** house"
Yerakot **oo** *feirot* / "vegetables **and** fruits"

Conclusion

Hopefully, you have enjoyed this book and will use the knowledge you have learned in various situations in your everyday life. In contrast to other methods of learning foreign languages, the theory in this current usage is that ever-greater topics can be broached so that one's vocabulary can expand. This method relies on the discovery I made of the list of core words from each language. Once these are learned, your conversational learning skills will progress very quickly.

You are now ready to discuss sport and school and office-related topics and this will open up your world to a more satisfying extent. Humans are social creatures and language helps us interact. Indeed, at times, it can keep us alive, such as in war situations. You might find yourself in dangerous situations perhaps as a journalist, military personnel or civilian and you need to be armed with the appropriate vocabulary.

"This is a base for military aircraft only," you may have to tell some people who try to enter a field you are protecting, or know what you are being told when someone says to you, "Welcome to the border crossing." As a journalist on a foreign assignment, you may need to quickly understand what you are being told, such as "The sniper killed the highest-ranking lieutenant." If you are someone negotiating on behalf of the army, you may need to find another lieutenant very quickly. Lives, at times, literally depend on your level of understanding and comprehension.

This unique approach that I first discovered when using this method to learn on my own, will have helped you speak the Hebrew language much quicker than any other way.

NOTE FROM THE AUTHOR

Thank you for your interest in my work. I encourage you to share your overall experience of this book by posting a review. Your review can make a difference! Please feel free to describe how you benefited from my method or provide creative feedback on how I can improve this program. I am constantly seeking ways to enhance the quality of this product, based on personal testimonials and suggestions from individuals like you. In order to post a review, please check with the retailer of this book.

Thanks and best of luck,

Yatir Nitzany

www.ingramcontent.com/pod-product-compliance
Lightning Source LLC
Chambersburg PA
CBHW050334120526
44592CB00014B/2179